Riding at Anchor

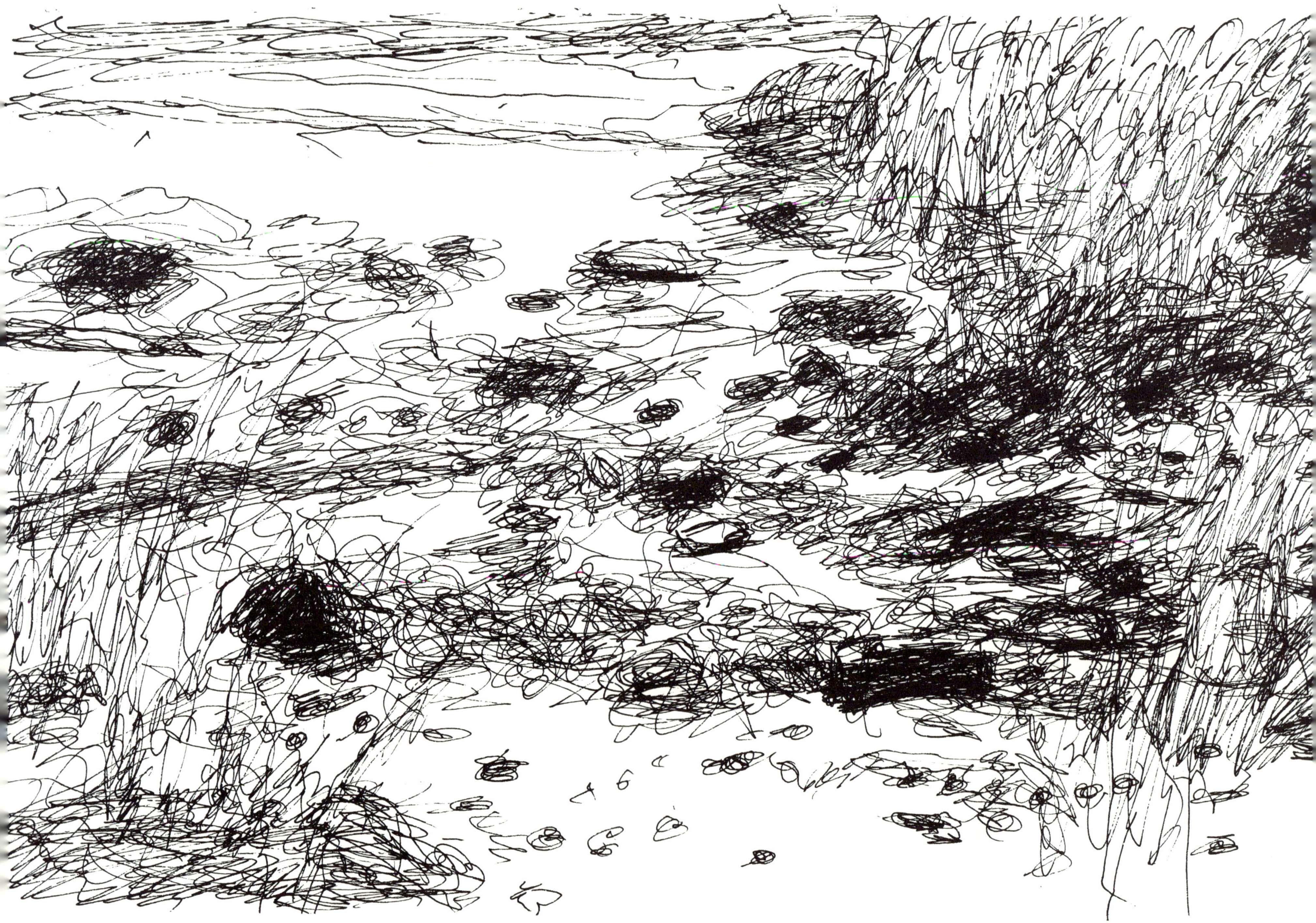

Riding at Anchor

Poems by Claire Nicolas White

Drawings by Stan Brodsky

With a Foreword by J. R. Schubel

Waterline Books
GREAT FALLS, VIRGINIA

This is a **Waterline** *Coastal Arts* Book

WATERLINE BOOKS
438 River Bend Road
Great Falls, VA 22066
(703) 759-0368

All rights reserved. No part of this book may be reproduced or used in any manner whatsoever without written permission except in the case of brief quotations for articles and reviews.

ISBN: 0-9628492-3-5

Copyright © 1994 Claire Nicolas White and Stan Brodsky

Production: Susan Spinney

Design and Composition: Julia Runk Jones

"Riding at Anchor" 1, 4 and 5 appeared in *Confrontation;* "Whirligig Beetle" and "Talking to God" in *Footwork;* "Port Jefferson Ferry" in *Live Poets;* "Swimming Among Swans" in *LIPS;* "History" in *Green Prints;* "Homecoming" in *Primavera* and *A Contemporary Reader for Creative Writing*

First Printing 1994

ACKNOWLEDGMENTS

We wish to thank the J. M. Kaplan Fund, Mr. and Mrs. Dennis Krusos and Cecily Pennoyer, whose generous contributions have made this book possible.

Contents

Foreword	6
Winter On The North Shore	8
Nissequogue River	13
Riding At Anchor	15
Talking To God	18
The Whirligig Beetle	22
Captivity	26
Company	28
The Span	30
Romance	32
Summer	34
Amphibian	36
Seduction	38
Swimming Among Swans	40
History	42
Japanese Maple	44
Telephone Pole	48
Port Jefferson Ferry	50
Homecoming	54
About the Author and Artist	56

Foreword

IN POEMS AND DRAWINGS, Claire Nicolas White and Stan Brodsky have captured the color, dynamism and changing moods of Long Island's coastal environments, an ecosystem more diverse than any area of comparable size in the United States, perhaps in the world. Poet and artist describe Nature's role as sculptor. They eloquently evoke the ephemeral beach art that is rearranged and revised by every tide, and the bottom-dwelling organisms of the Nissequogue River estuary alternately exposed and drowned by these tides. For there is much more to Long Island's shores than their readily apparent natural beauty.

From the ocean-battered beaches, to the relatively quiescent shallow expanse of the Great South Bay, to the craggy bluffs of the North Shore — all of Long Island's coastal features are young, most only a few thousand and all less than ten thousand years old. These features were formed by the most recent rise in sea level that accompanied the last retreat of the continental glaciers beginning about eighteen thousand years ago. All are dynamic and rapidly changing.

Relatively few species can tolerate the stressful conditions characteristic of near-coastal environments, but those that do are found in greater abundance, area for area, than in any other part of the world's oceans. Estuaries like Long Island Sound and the Great South Bay are among the most productive on Earth, far more productive than areas of intense agriculture. The impressive diversity of these environments makes learning about the processes that formed and continue to shape them a rewarding, challenging and humbling experience.

For more than four hundred years, this region has been one of the most densely populated in all of North America. White's descriptions of clorox bottles, crushed beer cans and plastic wraps stranded on Long Island beaches are graphic reminders of the sometimes uneasy relationships Long Islanders have with their natural surroundings, relationships that have grown more intrusive and problematic with increased population growth. And it is the intense and often conflicting uses of these environments by a large number of people that make this the greatest laboratory in the world for developing and testing strategies to allow humans to live in harmony with Nature. Coastal scientists, managers and policy makers are just beginning to exploit the special qualities of this remarkable laboratory. Ultimately however, it is society — all of us who care — that will determine what values and uses of these coastal resources are most important. The question remains whether we will have the commitment to implement the strategies needed to conserve those values and uses.

This book is an important addition to the literature of Long Island's coastal environments, a literature that matches these environments neither in variety nor in richness. Perhaps Claire Nicolas White's and Stan Brodsky's splendid volume will stimulate other Long Island artists to devote their talents and attention to the marine landscape. At least it will help readers to get better acquainted with our coast's beauty and to experience and understand its contribution to the quality of life. For me a trip on the Port Jefferson Ferry will never be the same.

J. R. Schubel
Dean and Director
of the Marine Sciences Research Center
State University of New York at Stony Brook

deep green

Brown

brown

yellow greens

Winter on the North Shore

I

The shrouded land
mirrors itself
a dark mass
of marsh in mist
its double image
swallowing
all sound

clumps of mounds
hirsute with reeds
still as asleep
bent on their own reflection
float on banks
of opaque light
beyond

II

Bulbous white Clorox bottles
aniline blue and yellow
plastic wraps
crunched metal beer cans
clash with soft edges
gray brown   washed with rain
cling to beach plum branches
black against bleached sand
and dry grasses that obey
seasonal withering

veils of saran wrap
hang from trees
like ghosts of birds fled
sing despair   flutter there
in naked winter's flat white light

III

There is no rhyme or reason
to the rhythm of the stones
along the shore
escaping counterpoint or pattern
they defy design
define the natural that can
erase the order we impose
on this chaotic randomness

We have clustered stars up there
to represent a scale   a bear
but should we rearrange the stones
to fit a scheme   the tide would come
at once to tear apart
the logic of our art

IV

In milky blue light
of winter thaw
ice floes capped with snowy crests
float by like swans
and creaking   break

opaque or thin as glass
quick waters ripple
wind their lively paths between
jostle   dissolve and trap
music inside their light

Birds flap and draw
their loops in tender air
weave longing cries with distance
then descend to settle
in colonies   still as prayer

V

No boom of waves here
no pretense at voicing
great messages
only this nibbling seeping
teasing brackish water
that creeps up and down
swallowing salt hay
lifting stones deposited
further   falling away
leaving us disorder and decay

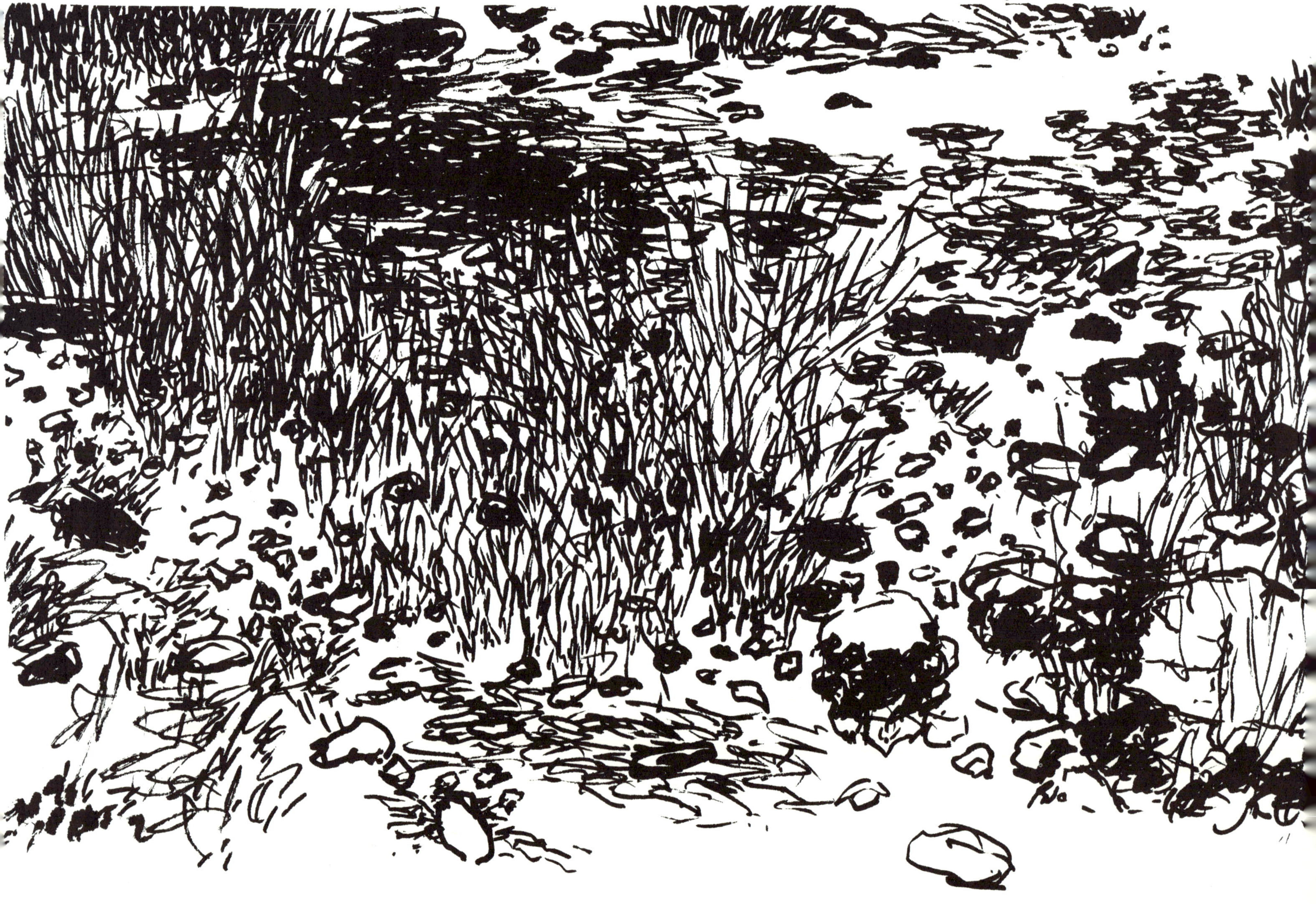

VI

Pushed to the edge
we'll fall off into space
suddenly there is room
for wings
only gods walk on water
and though beaches obey
gravity
and coasts blur distance
it is the horizon
that incites to flight
that draws away
from this daedalus
this tangle of scurrying tracks
keeping traffic
locked inland

VII

Reaching the end
we meet the depth of air
and the cold bay
to explore further
would take gills
or anti-gravity

Water reflecting sky
locks its secrets
in this mirage
implies profundity
knows how to tantalize
with the unknown

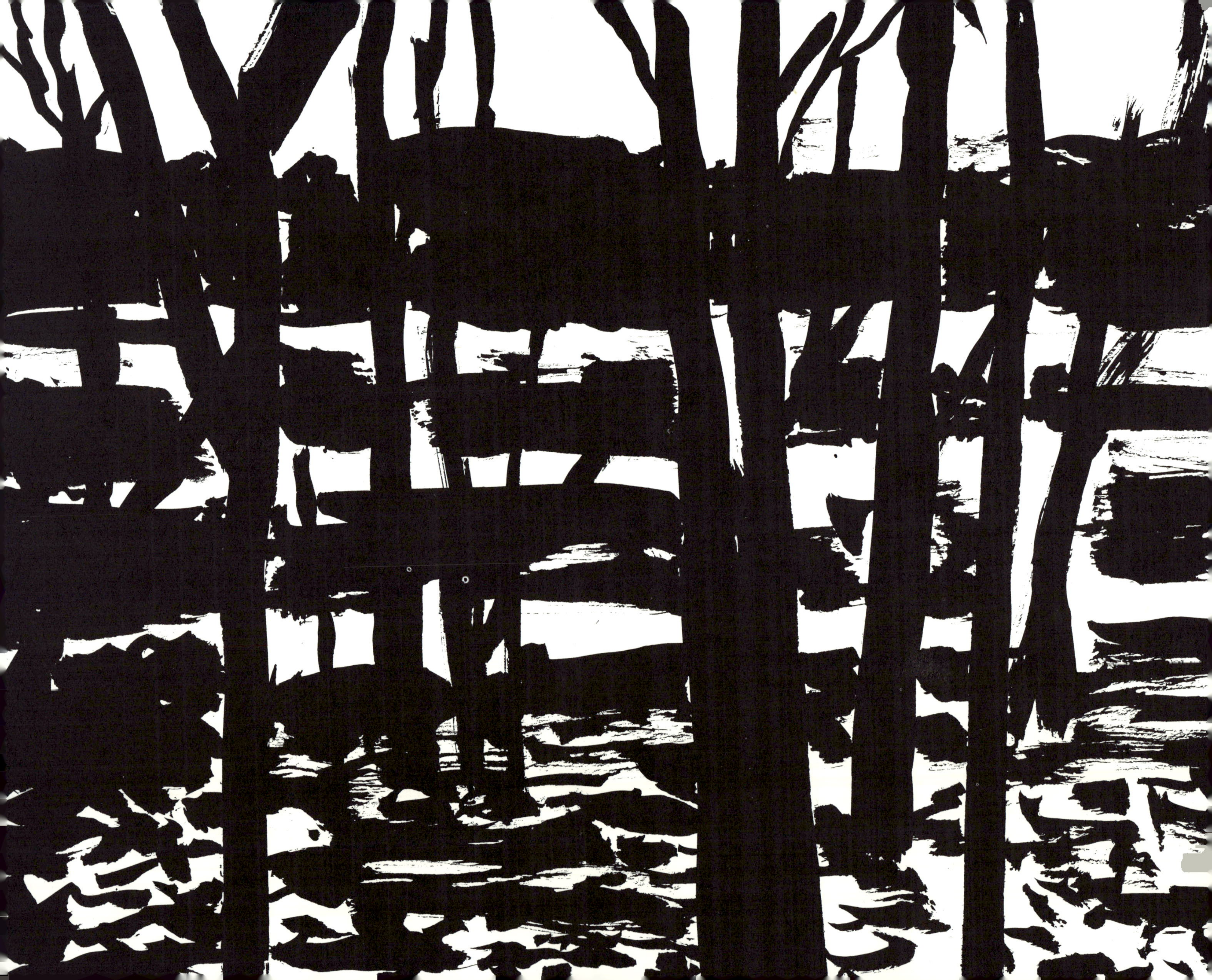

Nissequogue River

When the tide seeps out
the mud's route winds
through a high, channeled
labyrinth of reed forests
rooted in layers on layers
of breathing bivalves
and crab tenements oozing
sea sweat, black glue
building this metropolis
hard-shelled, creature crawling
and alive with a spitting
sliding, tentacled
mollusk population

Herons, curtain-winged
glide here in silvery silence
swoop through the avenues
stand immobile on banks
with long, curved necks
while egrets hang
in ghostly clusters
on water-rooted willows
all waiting in evening's
still descent for the pull
of the water rushing now
away, exposing the roots
of this underworld

Riding at Anchor

I

St. James Episcopal Church,
the prow of a ship, sails

trailing its cargo of graves
across the field to the sea

to drown it in the deep,
to sink it in oblivion.

Those who will not accept
a steeple as their captain

or this fate of fertile sleep
on a familiar shore

pull up their moorings, drift,
fight the pull of tides,

feel the tug of trains,
buy one-way tickets West,

flee the drowning coast,
become a weightless freight,

a restlessness of ghosts
that cling to speed and clamor.

And I shall wave at these
light-hearted travelers

longing to emulate
their unencumbered flight,

with one foot in the grave,
and one foot on the track.

II

You and I, in our robes,
our coats of time
that grow thicker, darker,
gather around us dream furnishings,
pockets stuffed with years, secret moments sewn
    in seams,
lined, buttoned, zippered tight,
keeping us warm when in the distance
sounds a cold wind.

Around us departures
stir in the night,
but the weight of our density
falls like a stone,
like an anchor in what is to come.
We will be immovable,
heavy, to be torn
out of this ground,
a toxic deposit
eroding the basement
of this house.

III

Wounded dogs
stay close to the ground,
wrap themselves in the landscape
they know like a great-coat.
The rivers they once fished,
the woods they roamed,
the mountains they climbed,
the seas in which they swam
now feed their twitching sleep.

Wounded men
wind clocks that drip
their minutes through the void,
tap barometers that rise and dip,
verify events in other's lives,
read histories in which
to situate their own,
married to their pain
on which they lean like a cane,
a perfect couple.

IV

When the roof falls in
there is still the sky

When the river rises
we'll take the boat

When the boat sinks
we'll learn to swim

When there's no more wine
we shall change the water

What the CAT scan knows
is hidden by skin

When the hour comes
can we make it sweet?

V

The country of no return
    Is it this near?

A dark season
in which islands of light
    punctuate
my progress, driving away
    from home

a circle of water surrounds me
    it is magic
keeping the wind at bay

I haul in the road behind me
    and abandon land
for the light in the night
    not a trace
of regret for the ties
    that bind

Here I am new to myself
    light as a ship
without cargo and without anchor
    or destination

Could it be as simple as this
    to disappear?

Talking to God

You have a right
to do what you do
not being a democrat
but allow me to mention
a certain peevish vengefulness
in the teasing accidents
you invent for the long-suffering
the worm for instance that you sent
to eat the leaf that shaded
Jonah as he rested
outside Nineveh
and the way both our cars broke down
the day our trials were to end
if only we could get away

No wonder you have few friends!

Was it you who introduced
the word that ends all arguments
bends the knee and bows the head
amen?

Years go by and you forget
to remind us life is meant
to be barren
it grows opulent with weeds
hirsute with spiked blossoms
leaves the size of hats
babies pop out of every cabbage
forests grow back
the earth heals its scars
rain washes pain
suns rise, moons tumble, a juggle of stars
spins over stinking cities
where somehow traffic keeps moving
inexhaustible as your energy

Seven years of plenty
followed by you know what!
Every earthquake gets us
every germ hits home
at the meat counter all I hear
is tales of medical interventions
violent wrenchings that turn the body
inside out   meant to prolong
life indefinitely so we forget
our own mortality

The epitaph that sticks in the throat
hurled at one by the pious   oh
whatever you are not "merciful"
mercy implies gratitude
due you in spite of havoc
and error and cruelty
I shall not be meek with you God
let us both admit our faults
you are vengeful and aloof
I am rebellious and prickly
You sent your son
to be spat upon   murdered
is that the way to treat
one's only child?

Then suddenly   in the ugly church
where loudspeakers drone
the hi-fi system squeaks
and the Irish lady sings
"infihinihit thy vast dohomain"
it rains on me   an easy prey
and you win again   in your embrace
I melt in a dazzle of grace

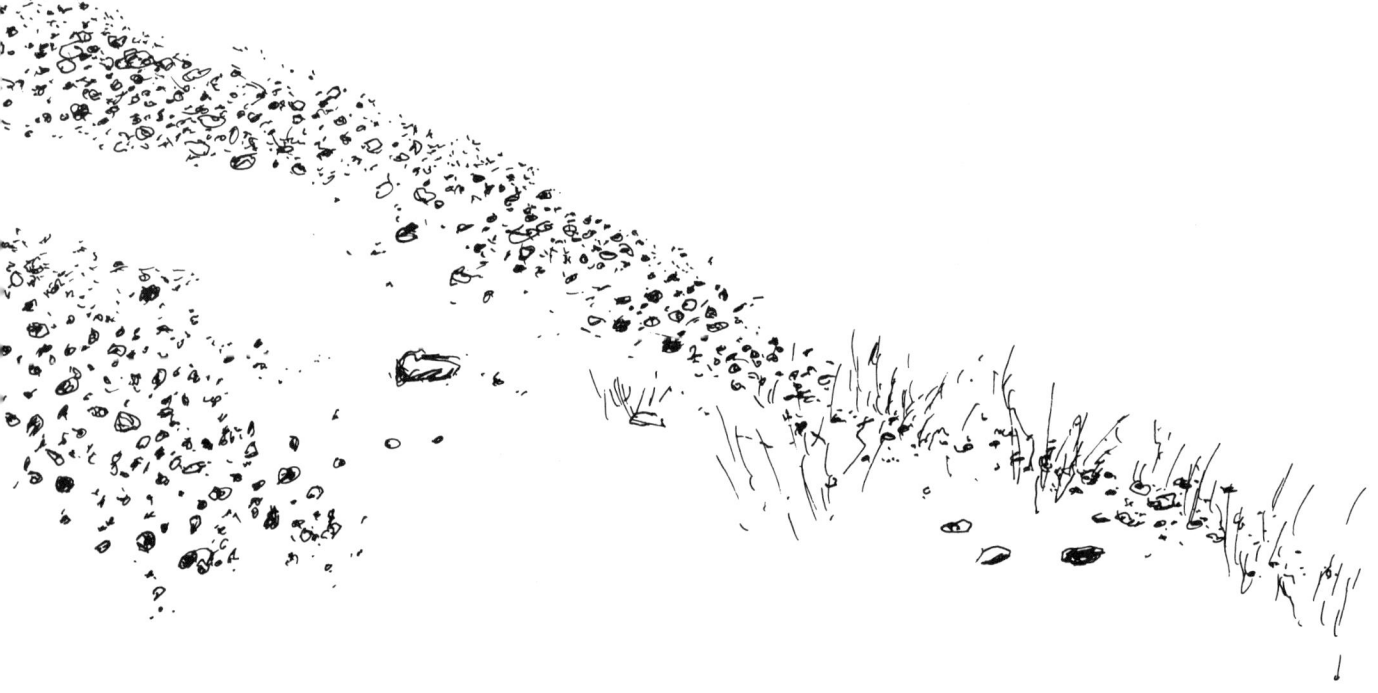

Stan Brodsky
1977

The Whirligig Beetle *A Sonnet Sequence*

I

An endless chain of gestures links this one
with other days. I move while standing still
like treading water, say, or climbing on
a downward escalator, while the kill-

er has his eye on me and takes his time,
seeing me out of breath and frantic like
a mindless insect under a raised hand.
My aim meanwhile is just to find what rhyme

or reason all this has, or if I can
for one brief instant hold my gesture when
it is perfection, and there freeze.   The blow
will then deliver me.   I'll never know
the sequel, caught in a brief flash of grace,
a snapshot fixing me in time and place.

II

A restless beetle dances on the black
water of streams and ponds.   In my home tongue
its name is "Writer," though its dimpled track
leaves no more trace the minute it is gone.

Its English name is whirligig, which shows
proper contempt for an activity
that bears no fruit.   Yet, as this insect goes
about its business, my proclivity

to puzzle over anything that's crypt-
ic and obscure gives meaning to its script.
Its name written in water, does it spell
out all I really care about, and will
it save my own from anonymity,
or drown it in a smooth, unriddled sea?

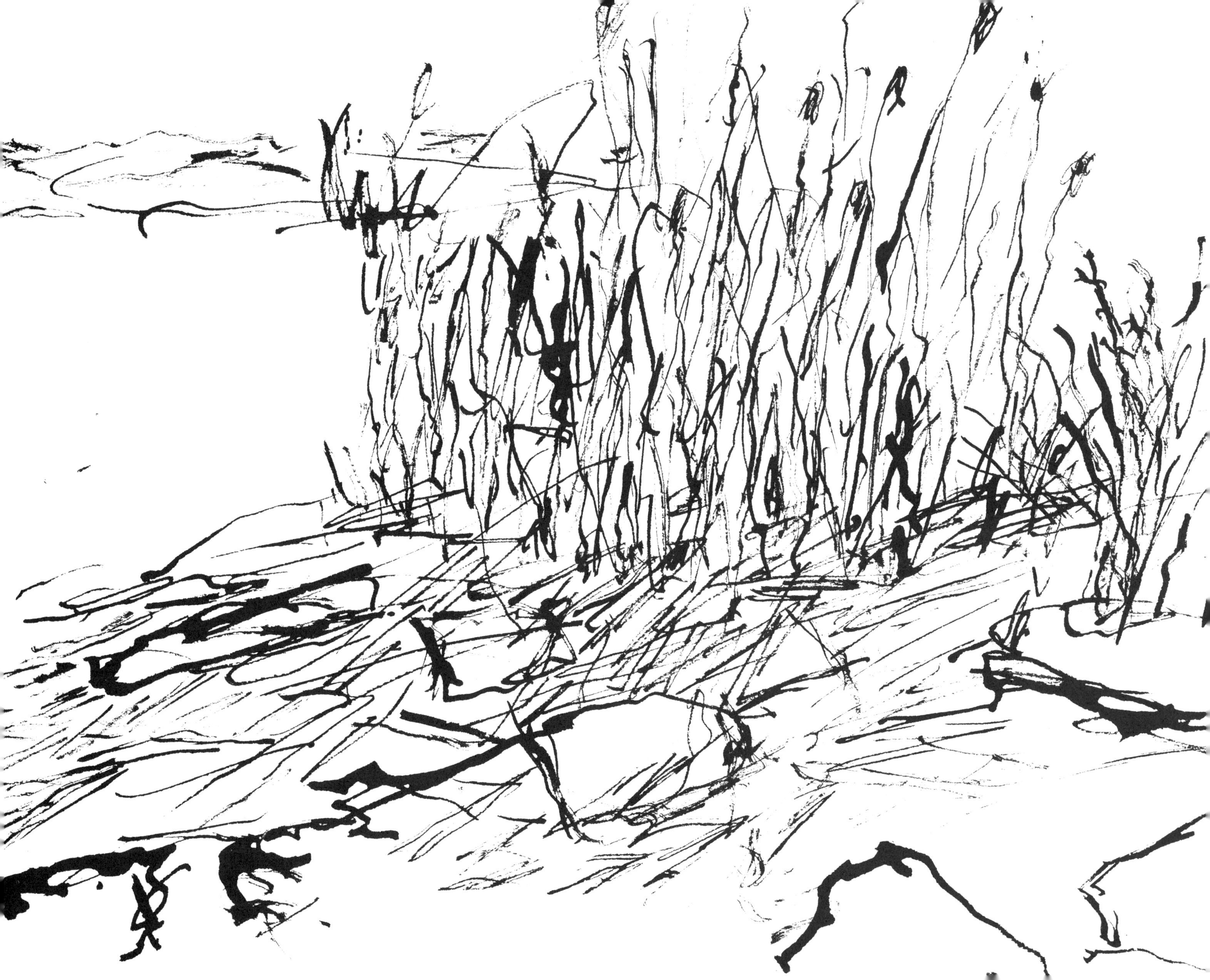

III

No matter. Through the windows of my room
I watch the light. It blazes in the West
behind a grid of trees, and all too soon
it etches the horizon with a crest

of orange. Then the moon will lick the deep
transparent sky. This is my nest of dream
woven year after year with words, to keep
track of the days, a sieve in which to glean

a pittance for my ego. Anyone
is welcome to this legacy: a stone,
a leaf, a pale hieroglyph. Transform
it as you will.   Blow whispers into storm,
invent a personage as complex as
you wish, so long as you record, "She was."

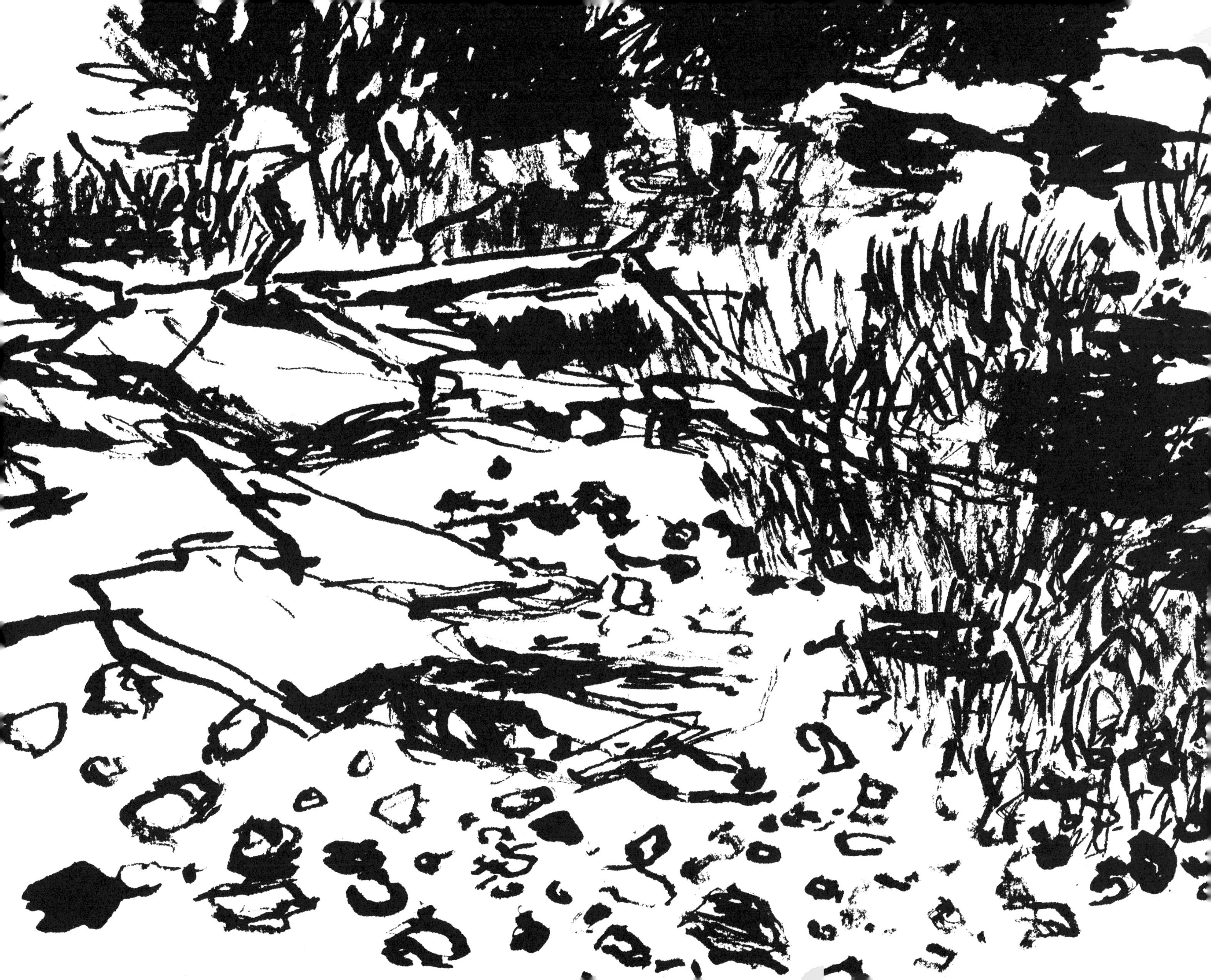

Captivity

The winter boats
are landed now
tethered to houses
birds without wings
caged between trees
out of their element

Domesticated they stand
in wraps   dreaming of feet
on which to run away
awkwardly top heavy
dwarfing the little houses
that hold them in tow

From the kitchen window
the women keep an eye on them
while the men in their stocking feet
sit in the parlor
dreaming themselves
afloat

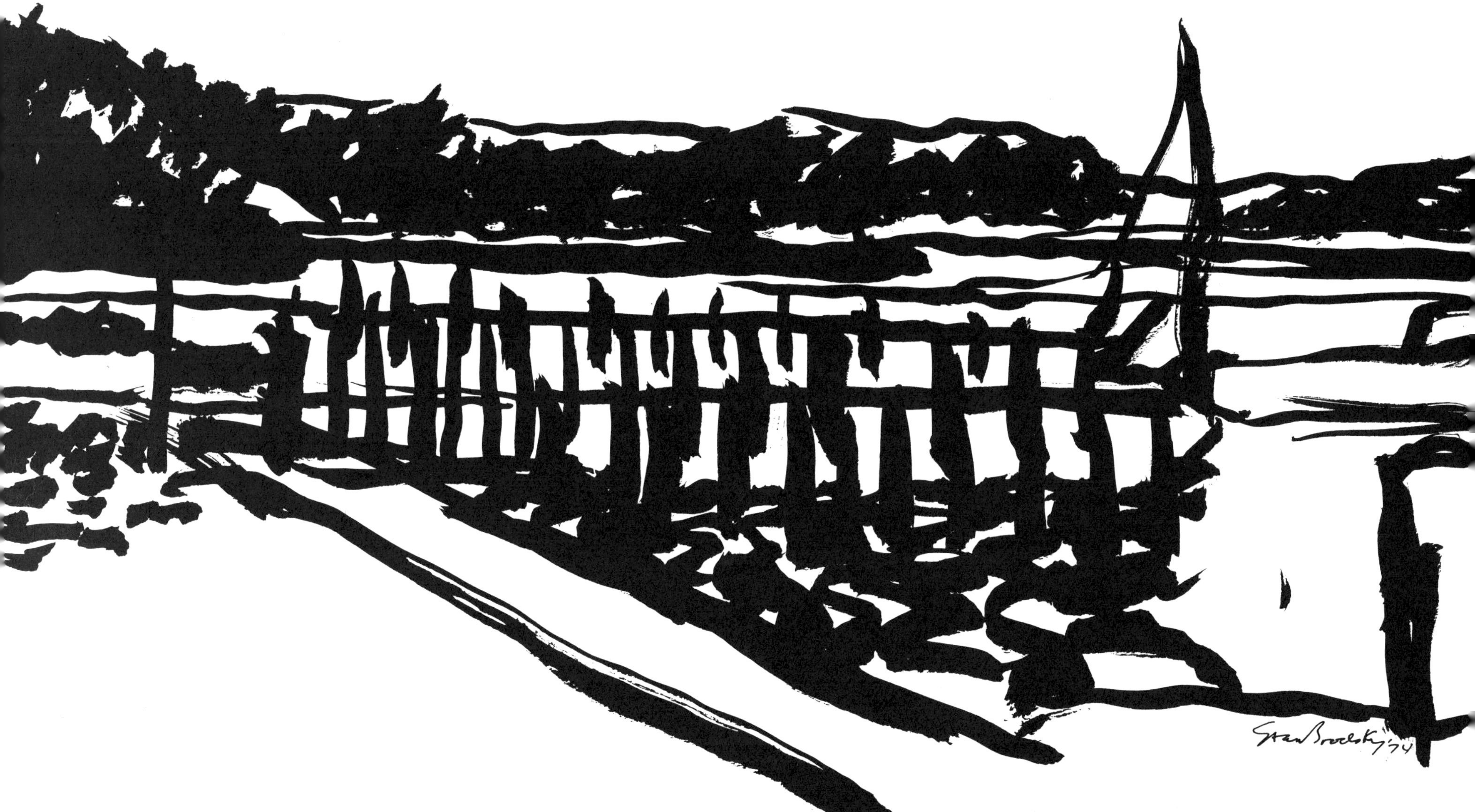
Stan Brodsky '74

Company

In a land of beasts
bleat, cackle and grunt
of grubbing sow
delight the melancholy misanthrope.
These sad submissive creatures
wearing sun or rain in their fur
or iridescent feathers
how well they understand our sorrow
head lowered to near-sighted nourishment.

Pasture gives way
to cess and swimming pool.
Three horses in my paddock
haloed by winter sun
stamp their hooves
on frozen soil
wait in line like Russians
for hay. They pay no rent
but wake me with a sudden burst of gallop.
What lonely joy stirred them
to greet the New Year with a dance?

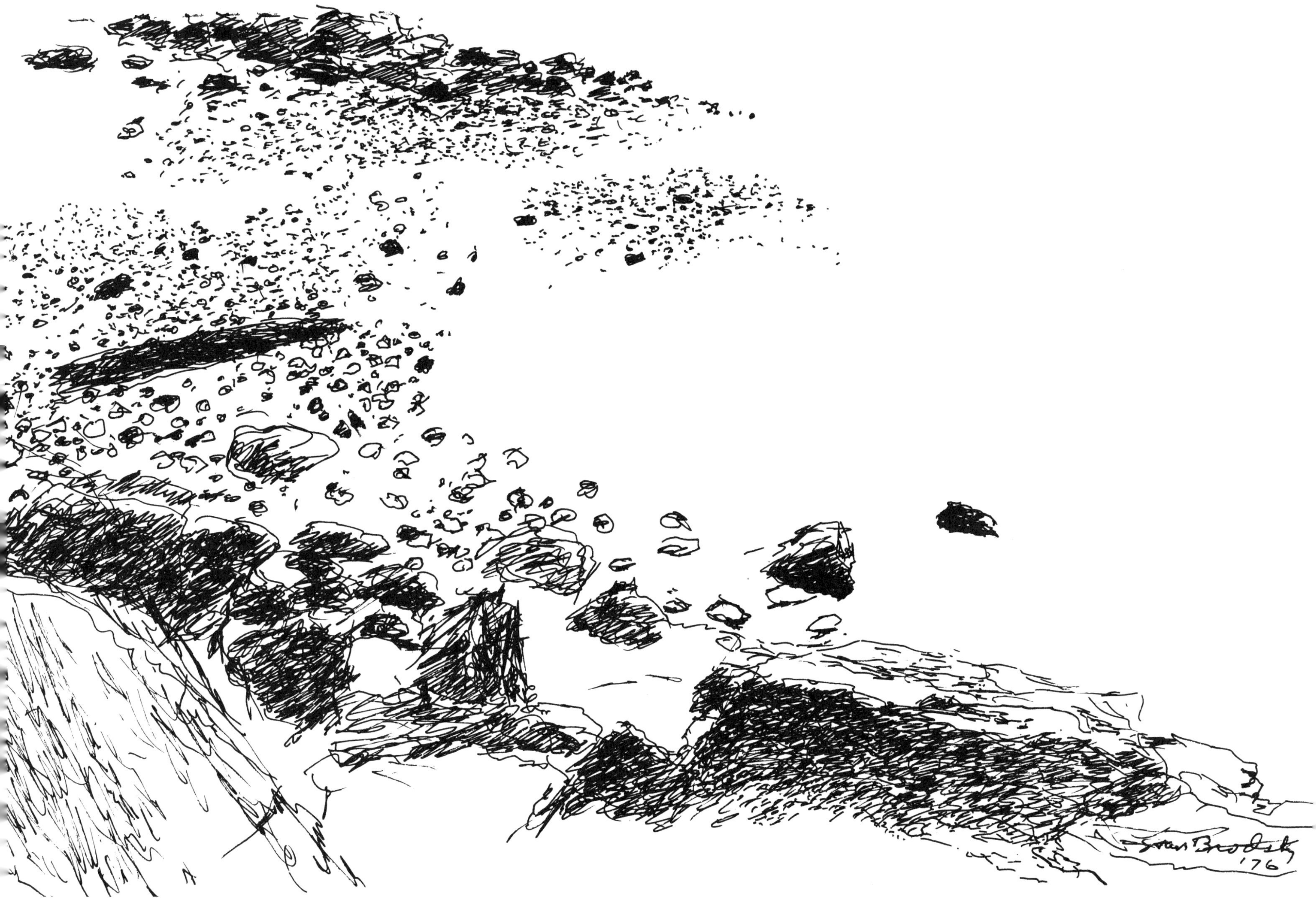
Stan Brodsky
'76

The Span

In the house in the North long ago
when night fell, we went wrapped in wool
down circular stairs. The halls
we crossed past tight-lipped doors
were dark and cold. At last
we came to a carpeted burrow
in which our ancestors sat
in the glow of lamplight and stove.

They taught us time to the still
hiss of flames. At their feet we played
with buttons in boxes, blessed
with natural silence, the safe
constant of beginning and end
in the deep house, under the weight
of stars, anchored by these
two shy benevolent moles.

Now we too become gravity's guests.
A child with a fever lies
in the room where I sew a seam
and fire sings in its hollow
belly. Wind rattles the baffles.
Then the child's breathing swells
lifting us out of our chairs
till we reach the brim of the world.

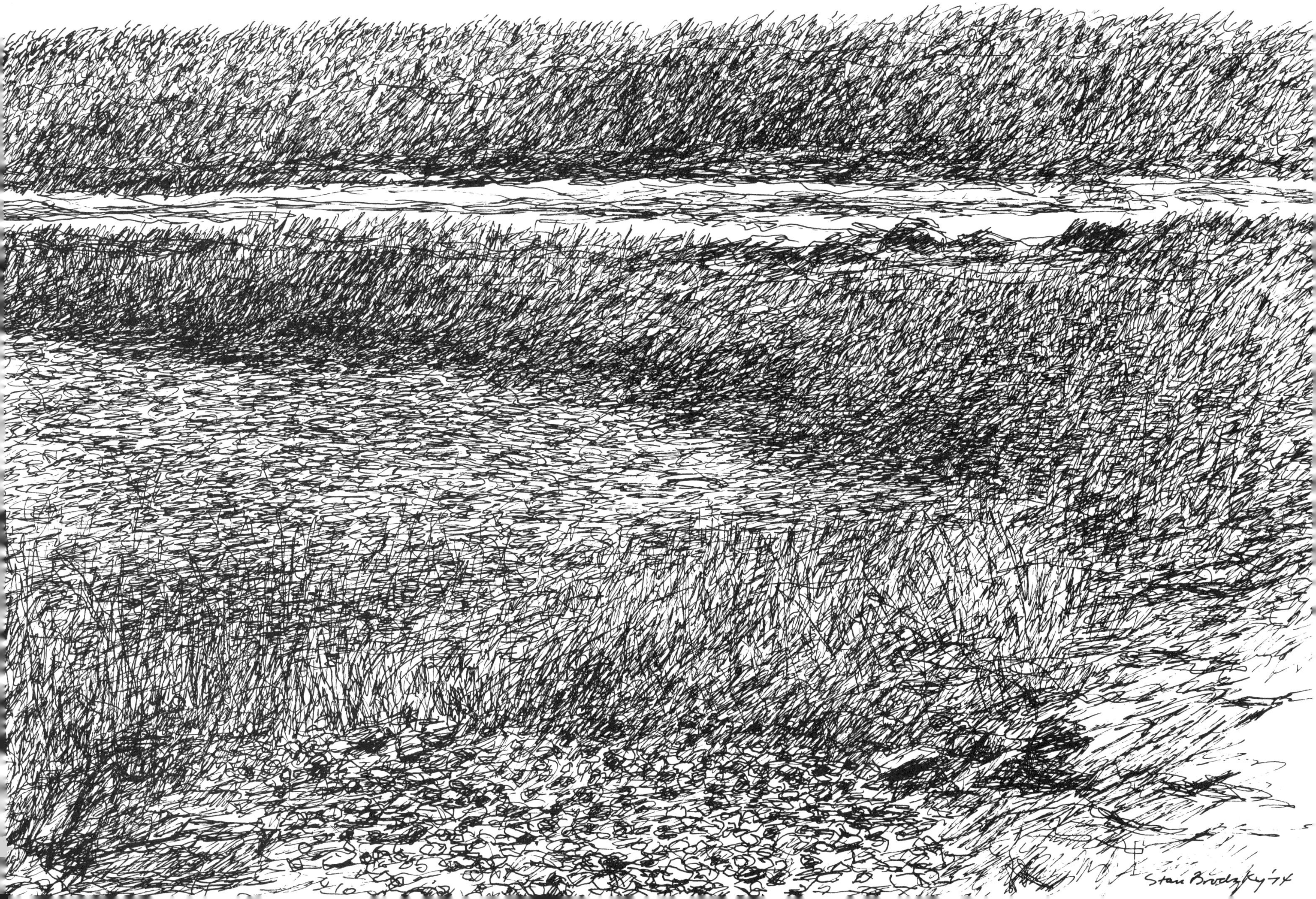
Stan Brodzky '74

Romance

    Late April.
I go down to the spring
where a spigot spits
its clear water out
from under the hill, at the harbour.
And yes, it is there again
a field of watercress
hiding behind skunk cabbage
under low branches
growing in thick brown mulch.
My boots squelch wet
as I cut spicy green leaves
careful not to uproot
their hairy white feet.

Who, while my back was bent
deposited on the stone
by the water spout
perfect, like a heart,
one red strawberry?
An angel? God? Clearly a gift
from some benevolent
silent passerby.
Rich with water and cress
I bless the donor of
this wealth, and eat.

Further down the road, I pass
a white-haired, sprightly man
walking a cocker spaniel
through a cloud of forsythia.
    Hey, I think it's him!
    A love affair!

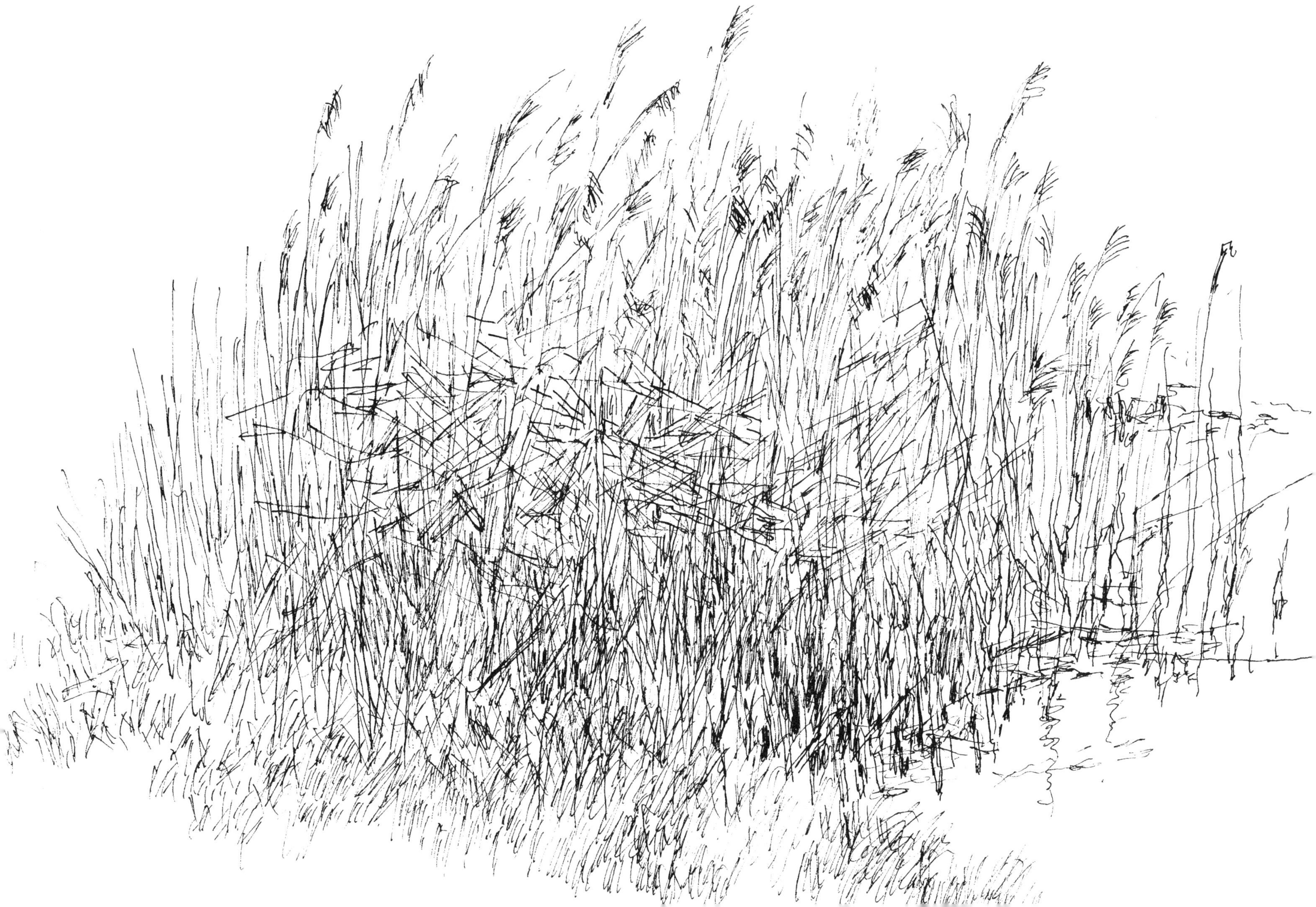

Summer

It is an orgy that makes me nervous.
The weather goes on and on
to be loved with continuous ecstasy.
But things interrupt, like calling the dentist.

The memory of summer intervenes
    with the present:
a picnic by the roadside in Pennsylvania,
driving a car full of sleeping children
    through moonlight,
water, its cucumber smell,
its blue window to shatter, its cool embrace
to gather around me.

But the desire exceeds the consummation,
the memory more vivid than the present.
Summer, rushing by uncaptured
restlessly burns away like grass.

Then comes the rain.
I sink into it with blessed torpor,
my bones heavy, my blood turning to mud.
The wind on its great wings erases sound,
wipes out all desire, all preconceived notion
of pleasure with the music on the panes
and the branches sweeping out there,
shaking their green hair.
Even the garden chairs forgotten
in the bower seem more blissfully fulfilled
with only rain sitting on them.

I lean out of the window, wishing I were
    a chair.

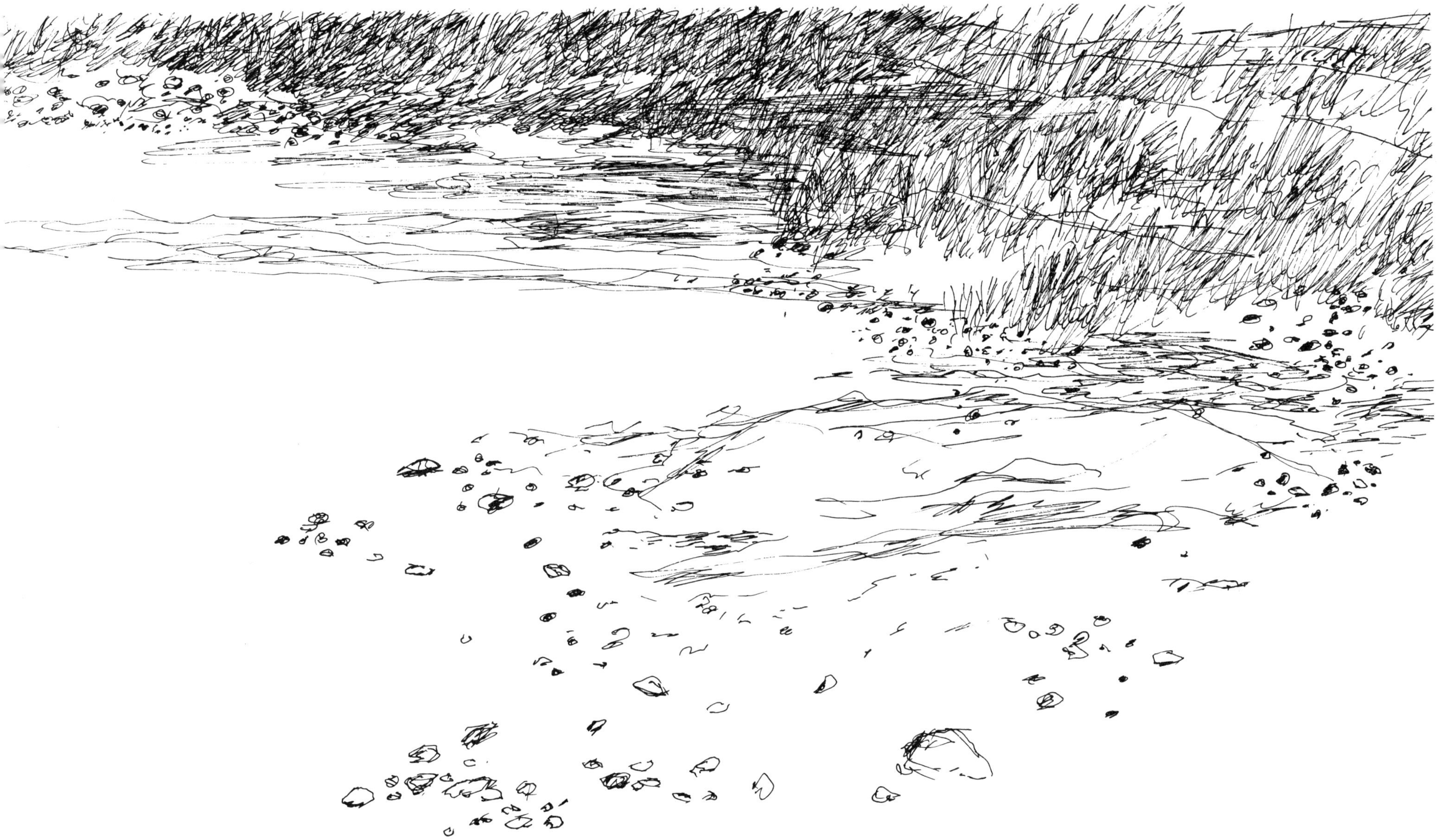

Amphibian

Solid water had fallen
past my window for days.
The roof miraculously held.
The walls remained impermeable
but sweating, moldy,
the light as green
as inside a bottle,
the sound a liquid panic
and I at its core
      dry.

It stopped. I stepped into the bottom
of an aquarium, the floor
spongy, the air a thick embrace.
My gills pumped. Vines
leapt at me, leaves the size of parachutes
swam like buoyant medusas
over my head.
A gummy rot attacked my feet
oozing brown muck.
The smell of oxygen
and fermenting leaves
prickled my eyes.
Silence clung to me.
Then, with a flick of a fin
I vanquished gravity.

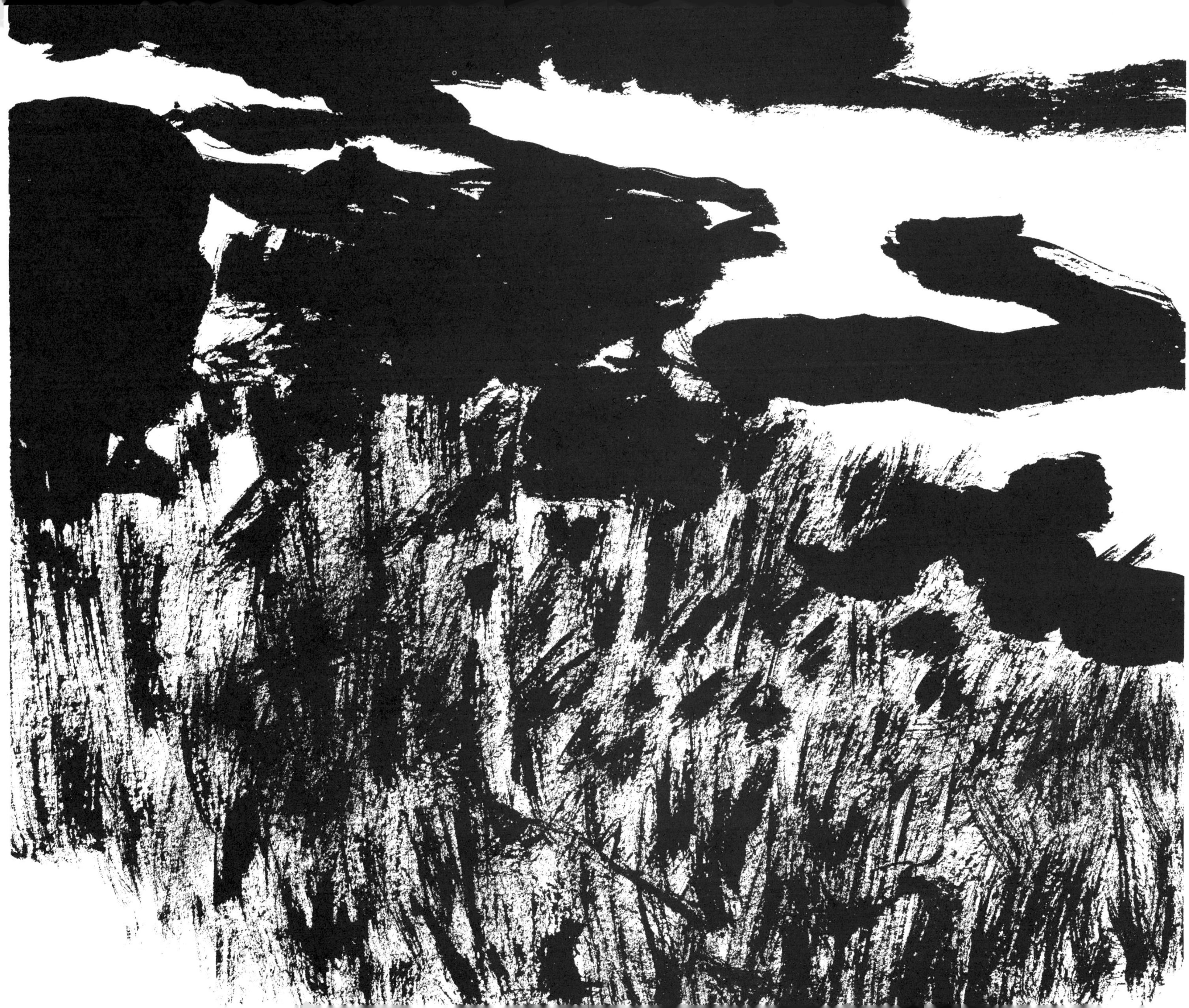

Seduction

The skin of the pool
taut as a veil
tears as I slip in
then weaves about me
a web of light.
Ravished
I'm trapped
in sun.

The beach, a perfect arc
of pebbles embraces
water in which float
viscous corollas
of medusas.
No matter where I go
water, my lover
prepares its sting.

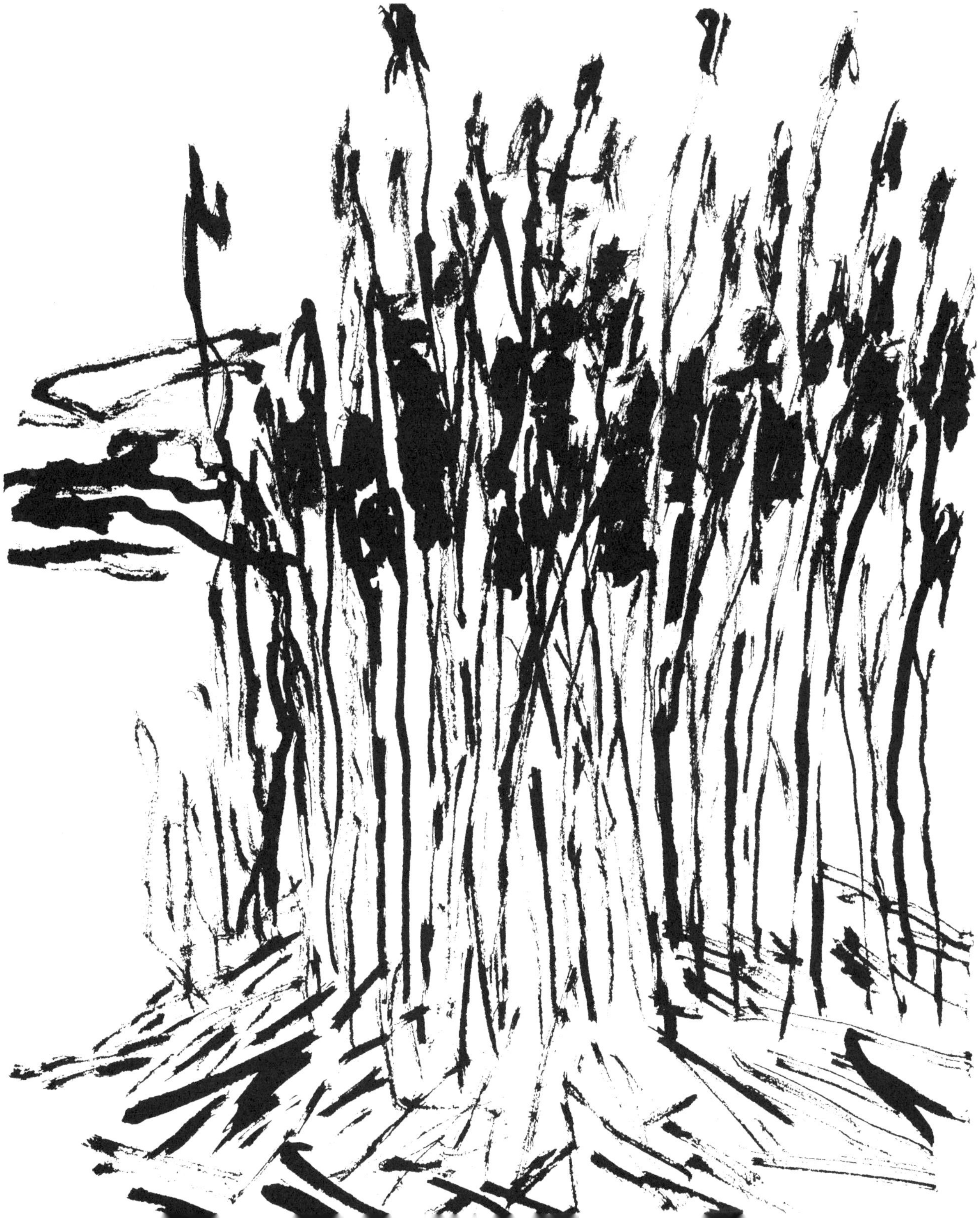

Swimming Among Swans

The first time I swam
at Cordwood Path beach
was at night, naked
with men, the fear
of their white skin
     near

Next only swans appeared
three of them, a mystic number
regal, rare
distant, not yet
     a threat

But like others swans multiply
to seven the next year
brother princes
bewitched in fairy tales
men underneath their
     feathers

Soon swimming became a risk
as I went down in Autumn
sunlight thin, water
a chill challenge, the coast
jealously guarded by dangerous
     dozens

They advanced towards me
along the dark sand
on ugly black feet
necks outstretched, spreading
the menace of their lethal
     wing clap

Oh Leda, easily over-powered
by the god grotesquely disguised
as fowl, I did not have
your stamina, and fled
     their embrace

We are going again to Little Men
but the path is narrow.
The barbed wire catches
at our summer dresses
as we reach for poppies
cornflowers and daisies
to bring to the man
who whistled, who whistled
so long ago in the Garden of the Lions.
The negative moon, driven by the wind
is snarled in the wires of the telephone pole.

Port Jefferson Ferry

I

    Glazed with sun
the gull-white ferry swallows whole
cars, campers, trucks, travelers
      into its black belly.

Slowly rotating, the ship
lowers its jaw
slides into lift-off
over the promise of pale blue sea
reflected onto the sky's surface.

All my desire sails with it.
I close my purse and drive
      inland
towards evening.

II

The voyage not taken
is an empty road through vineyards,
the festival in the village
come upon at an unexpected bend,
the smell of smoke from chimneys,
the brush burning on harvested fields,
the lonely man on horseback
carrying a dead pheasant
guiding me to the inn
at the end of the tree-lined driveway,
the meal served by a host without face,
the moon reflected in the moat outside the window,
the taste of foreign sleep,
the crack of sun between closed shutters,
voices in the courtyard
and bells ringing rituals
to waken unknown gods.

The road not taken
leaps across great rivers
that shimmer in the valley,
climbs into steep mountains
to abandoned cities
where goats live in the castle

and wild cherries pucker the mouth.
Water from the well
lies clear as glass
in my cupped hands.
The face reflected in it
is that of someone
I did not become.

And the ghosts encountered:
William the Silent where the bullet felled him,
George Sand guiding Chopin's hand
on the piano at Nohant,
Greta Garbo and Stokowski
leaning over the parapet
of the Villa Cimbrone,
Old Michelangelo wandering the streets,
muttering, "I have no rest,"
Clytemnestra and her eagle brood
screaming in the ruins of Mycene,
Jesus   on the shore
of Galilee.

They have not seen me.

If I spread my cloth
with red checks in Sounion,
crossroad of land, sea and sky,
will they come with their hampers
of smoked fish, their honey cakes
and wine the taste of dew?

Angels rising from between
the pages of my book,
sit down with me and eat
to prove your substance is
more tangible than words.
Smell the asphodel.
Your voices, lighter than bells,
scatter between the columns
that uphold the sun.

It will never be perfect.
You'll be wearing running shoes.
The sardine cans have no keys.
Byron scratched his name
        into the marble.

III

Here the ferry grows out of the dawn.
It swells, it looms
slowly raising its jaw
and connects with the dock.
Passengers within this whale's belly
never saw the white schooner,
the pregnant spinnaker,
the flag of the New Republic.

They emerge and scatter,
their journey of small importance,
the news they bring trivial,
their drunken gait on pitching decks
sober on steady ground.

Steve Brodsky '76

Homecoming

After falling asleep
in ten different rooms
in mountains, in plains,
facing East, facing West,

I wake in the dark
and grope for a light.
I stumble and fall
in the most foreign place

of all. Where is this
tall room of serene
whiteness, these floors
painted red, this smell
of clean sheets and woodsmoke?

Beyond, in a hall
with mysterious closed doors
and burnished oak chests
stairs descend to a house

filled with objects that creak
and glow in the dark.
This must be the ultimate
inn, where I landed

my mission fulfilled,
where the perfect decor
awaits me, reinventing
the life I inhabited
    all along

Claire Nicolas White was born in the Netherlands but has lived on the North Shore of Long Island since 1947. She has published a memoir, *Fragments of Stained Glass* (Mercury House, 1989); a novel, *The Death of the Orange Trees* (Harper and Rowe, 1963); a book of poems, *Biography and Other Poems* (Doubleday, 1981); and three poetry chapbooks: *The Navel* (Rome Daily American, 1969); *Here and There* (Street Press, 1977); and *The Bridge* (Cross-Cultural Communications, 1987).

Her poems, stories and essays have been published in *The New Yorker, Partisan Review, Paris Review, Confrontation, The New York Times, Newsday, Art News,* and *Vogue*. Several of her plays have been performed on Long Island and elsewhere in the U.S. She has translated several novels from the Dutch, and has taught writing to Long Islanders of all ages.

Stan Brodsky has exhibited extensively in New York City and elsewhere in the United States, Canada and Europe. His works are included in the Hecksher and Parrish Museums on Long Island, the St. Petersburg Museum in Florida, the Port Authority in New York City and in many private collections.

In 1991, Brodsky received the trustee's award for creative achievement from Long Island University, where he was a member of the C. W. Post Art Faculty for more than thirty years. That same year his work was the focus of a retrospective at the Hecksher Museum.

He has been awarded fellowships from the McDowell Colony, Yaddo and the Virginia Center for Creative Arts. In Manhattan he is represented by the June Kelly Gallery, where he will be featured in a one-person show in the coming year.

Now hundreds have taken over the harbour
when I attempt to swim they ignore me
the fluff of their feathers pollutes the water
Self contained they glide
    into their own
        shadow

History

June's high tide green
leaves in its wake
stalks of decapitated iris,
the rotting leaves of jonquils.
Now the rush of roses spells
hurry, hurry, catch this all
too brief summer, while a wave
of tiger lilies floods the roadsides,
American as disordered plenty.

Hydrangeas threaten, the drought
flattens out fields. Leaves
have their death in them.
The acid pink of phlox
and large hearted mallow
reach late August with
roses of Sharon in tow.
By now I know this progression by heart,
a series of continuous farewells.

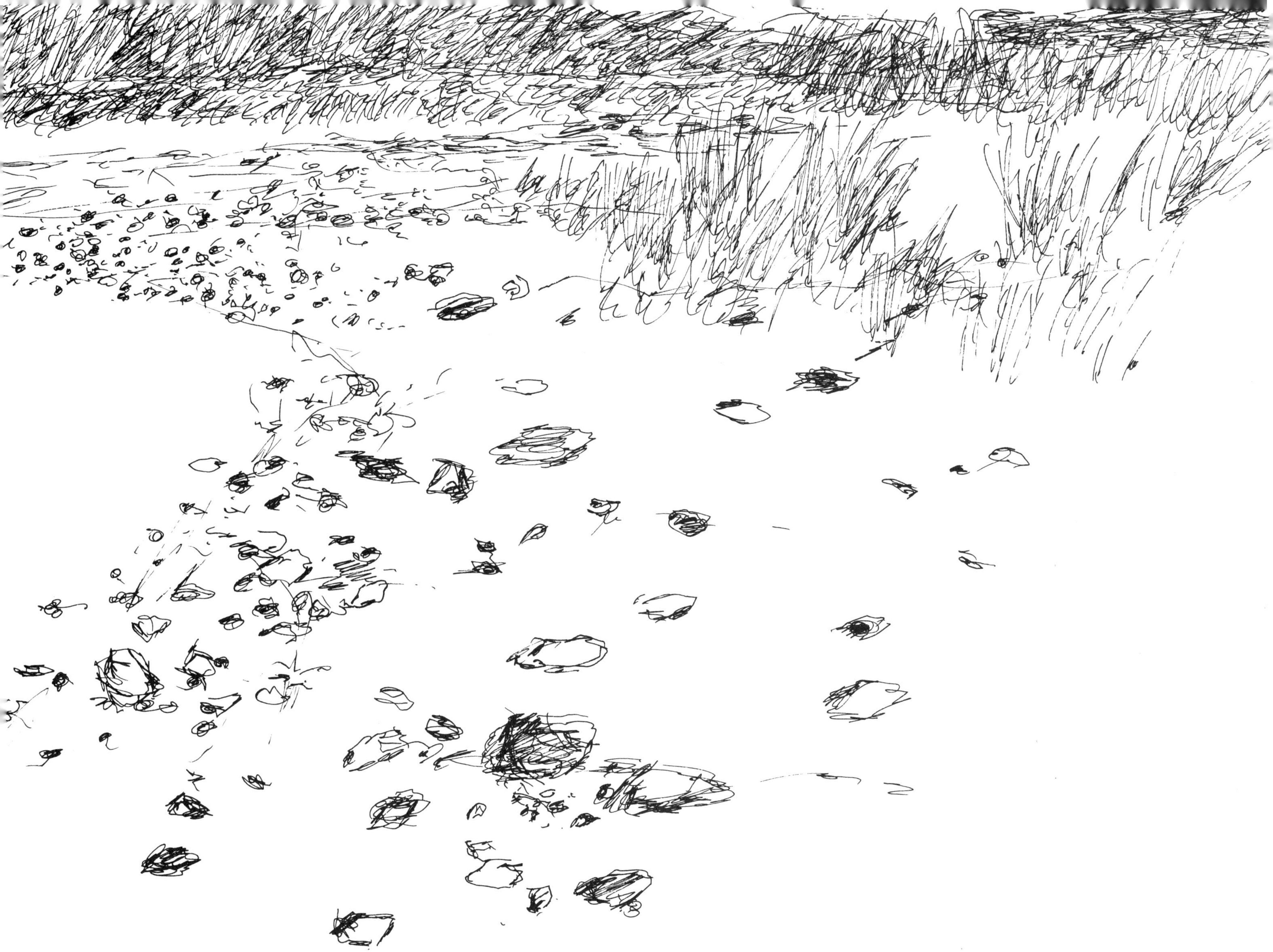

Japanese Maple

It starts at the crown
not flame or sunset red
but a furious blush such as
a woman's hair dyed crimson
when gray seeps in,
a mad dare, dizzying.

I catch it at it
from the second floor of the house
while still sedate below
but soon this tree in heat
can no longer hide
its hot flashes, its late
passion that explodes
in a garden grown cold.

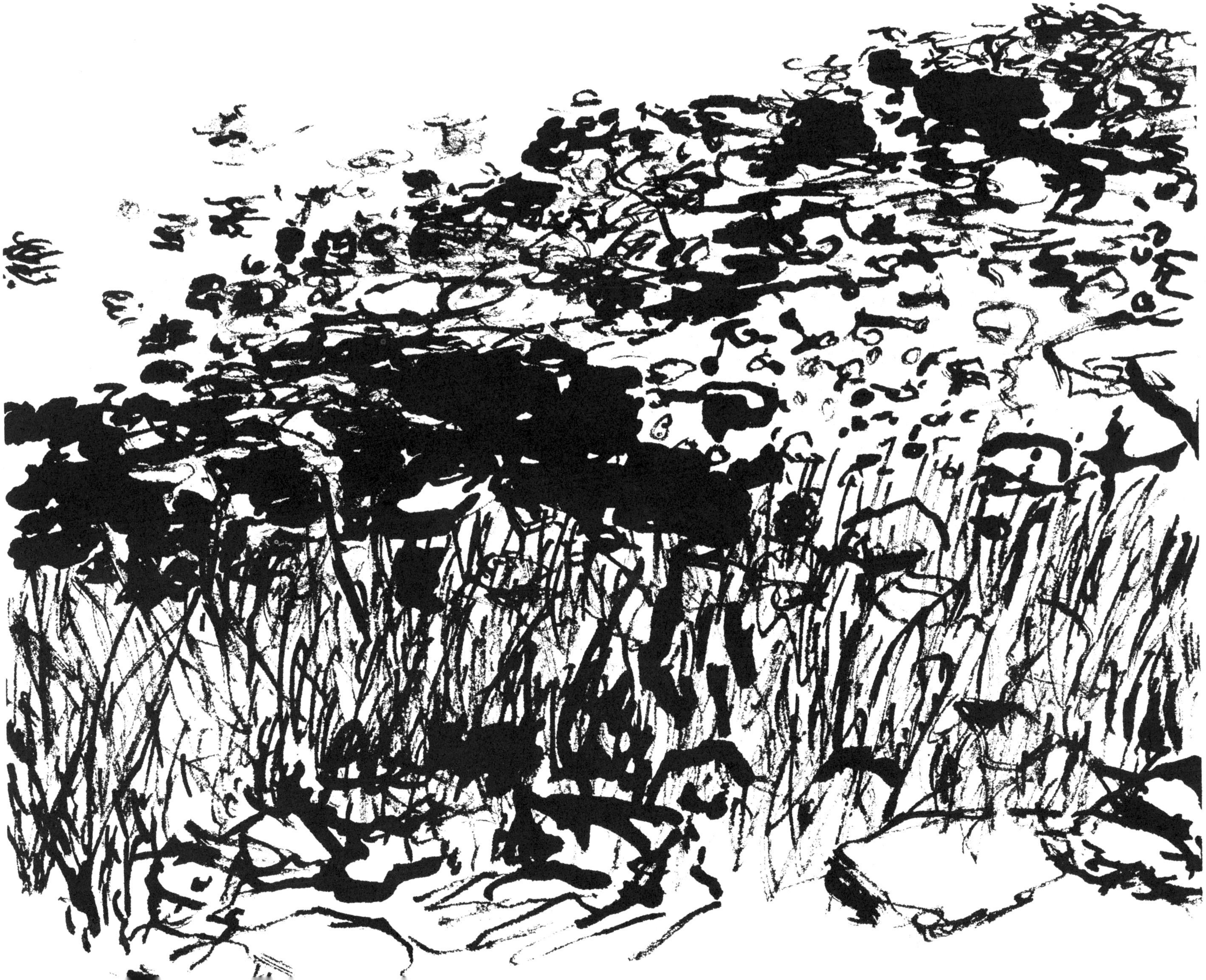

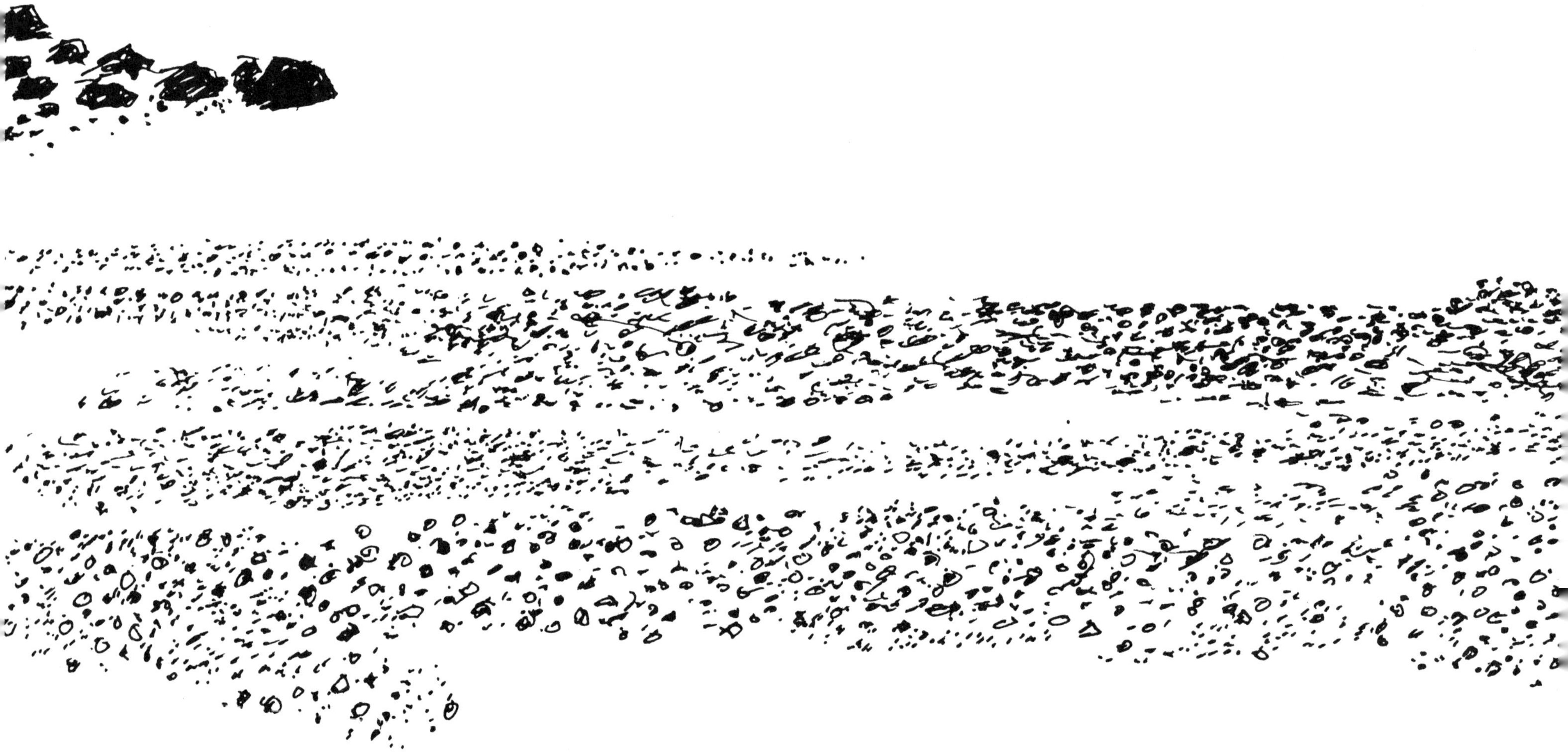

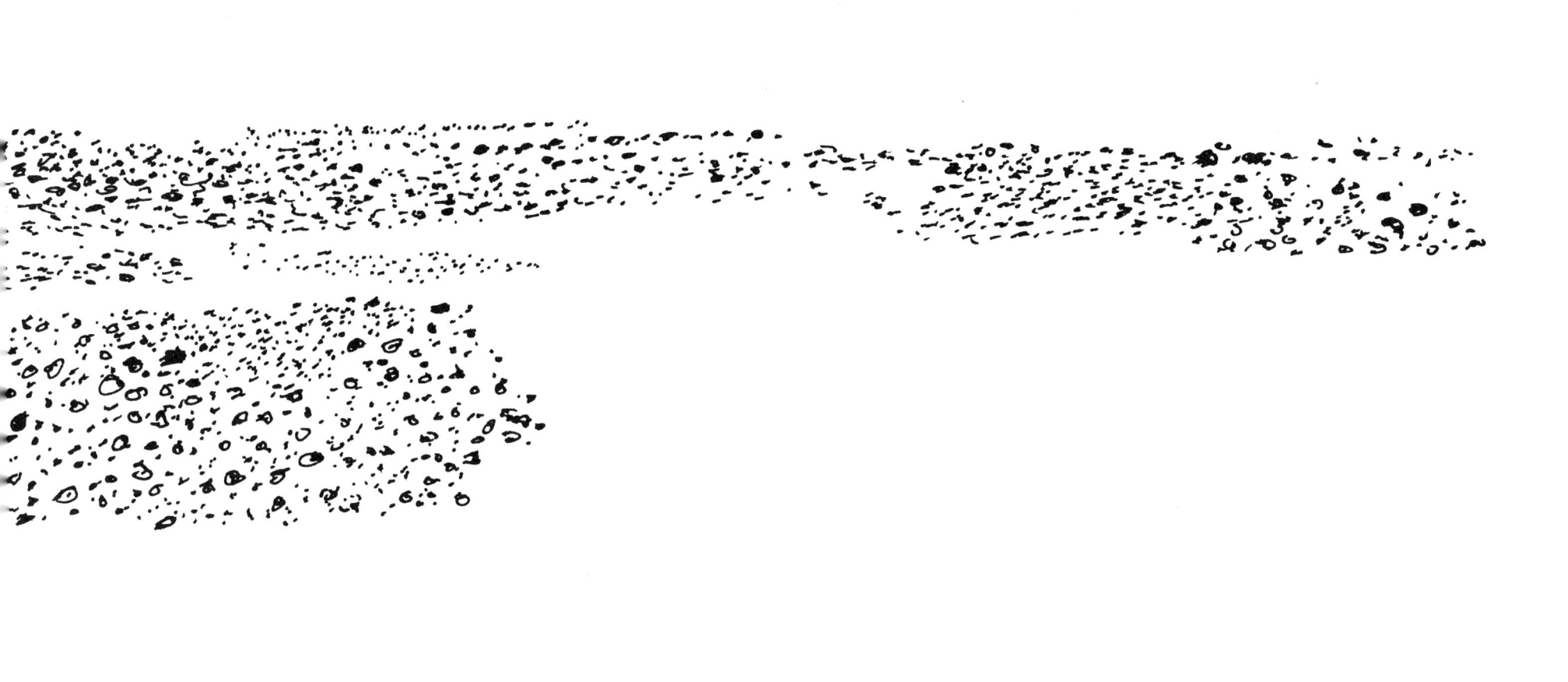

The Telephone Pole

Its black silhouette
outside my window
holds voices on leashes.
A wandering centaur howls
under a black moon.
The river burrows a hole
through the mountain
as it climbs back to its source,
a garden thick with paint and shadows,
the brown mush of earth
and rotting leaves.
Gliding behind the lyre-shaped trees
black with rain
a man passes. He whistles
three times. I follow him,
the river, the centaur,
to a wireless region where no messages
are left after the beep.

In the village called Little Men
they are bowling with thunder.
At the Inn of the Lions
glass bullets seal our bottles
and the painted ladies
walk beside the river
in their long trains. Their wings
drag in the mud.
Cakes big as wheels
glisten with gooseberries.
We step in bare feet
on patterns of rose petals
as the Eucharist passes
high over our heads.